JUSTINE WILSON

CRYSTAL
CONNECTION
A METAPHYSICAL STYLING GUIDEBOOK

Cover and internal design by Nada Backovic
Photography by Steffen Burggraaf-McCabe

NATIONAL
LIBRARY
OF AUSTRALIA

Cataloguing-in-Publication
entry is available from the
National Library Australia.

ISBN: 978-0-6487927-7-2
ISBN: 978-0-6487927-8-9 (ebook)

This book is dedicated to
my beloved mother Margot.

'Those who don't believe in
Magic will never find it.'
ROALD DAHL

CONTENTS

X

FOREWORD

Crystals can be clouded in mystery.

Many say that they hold a special energy, a power, an otherworldly vibration. This crystal magic has been harnessed for healing, meditation and rituals across cultures and around the globe for thousands of years. Crystals are a natural wonder, created over millions of years, incredible formations fused and moulded from the earth's rich elements.

Crystals are uniquely beautiful and intriguing. The way they catch the light, twinkle, shimmer and sparkle excites and attracts us. Whether you believe in their healing properties or not, don't be afraid to explore and discover a passion for crystals. Bringing them into your home can beautify and transform your space and add interest to your home environment. Crystals undoubtedly make beautiful and evocative visual statements within your space.

There is an emerging desire to incorporate these special stones into our abodes and a curiosity to understand the universal pull and appeal. Because of this I felt personally drawn to create this book. There is a surging awareness around wellness, mindfulness and new age beliefs, so it seems we are all searching for something more, maybe to just introduce a little magic into our experience again. Within these pages I showcase ways you can include these majestic mythical rocks into your home and personal environment, style them beautifully, and ultimately establish a relationship with them.

I like to call this movement, the *Crystal Connection*.

BEAUMARIS

MODERN

SIMON REEVES
ALISON ALEXANDER

FIONA AUSTIN

THE CONCEPT FOR CRYSTAL CONNECTION

Exploring crystals doesn't have to be overwhelming.
This book is designed to be an accessible place to start. The easiest way to find your own crystal connection is to start by surrounding yourself with crystals and see how you and your space respond. Whether it's through wearing jewellery, displaying crystal clusters, playing with small crystal stones or sourcing pieces of crystal decor, the best way to begin is by introducing them into your own personal realm.

As an interior designer, my love for crystals is just as much a visual affair as it is a spiritual one. I believe crystals hold healing properties and do change the vibration of the energy around us and the home. Crystals are simply beautiful! If your takeaway from this book is just an introduction, to source inspiration, or to indulge in a visual feast, I hope you gain some confidence to bring crystals close to you. If this is the end result, I will feel wholly fulfilled!

I must preface that I am not a crystal expert in the normal terms, meaning I do not know each of the exact minerals or properties that define each rock from a scientific standpoint, nor am I a master healer by any means. I do, however, have my own individual and powerful connection to crystals and have been drawn to collecting them for over 10 years. I enjoy the treasure hunt that is sourcing these beautiful stones. I feel the deep rush of adrenaline every time I find a crystal that I resonate with. It's quite frankly, a crystal addiction!

I hope to share what knowledge I do have around working with crystals with you. Also, as I incorporate them into my interior decor schemes and my own personal space, I hope you get some inspiration on how to display your special pieces too. It's important to note that there are many wonderful crystal guides and descriptive resources that are more encyclopaedic available. These books will quench your thirst and provide more information for individual stones. Please note, the intention of this book is to create more of a sensory and emotive visual guidebook, share my love for crystals and create some source inspiration. I will depict ways to style with and to connect to crystals in relation to your personal environment. By doing so, I hope to offer a new perspective on crystals and their ability to connect with you and your sacred home space.

GETTING STARTED

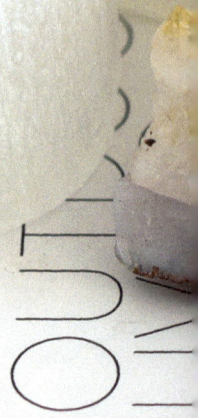

COCO REPUBLIC®

OUTDOO

OUTDo

EASY HOME STYLE

NEW YORK Christmas

OR LIVING

NIESCHLAG ★ LARS WENTRUP

Where to source crystals.
The best place to find crystals is at gift shops, markets, antique stores and dedicated crystals shops. Online platforms such as Instagram and Facebook also have a varied range of wonderful crystal sellers.

The best approach is to select a crystal that you are called to. I find in a sea of delectable choices, one crystal will always jump out. It could be the colour, shape or particular style that catches your eye. Please remember there are no right or wrong choices. Crystals come in many finishes such as raw, polished, clusters, points, pyramids, spheres, wands or other crafted unique shapes, small tiny samples to large statement pieces. There is no shortage of crystal options to choose from.

Generally speaking, any piece that has attracted you to pick it up, look closer, to touch and feel it, and ultimately to purchase it will absolutely work in your space. Just like any interior design selection, if you choose a piece you love it will become timeless. This approach also takes the stress out of knowing where to start. It is said that crystals can help with developing your intuition, your sixth sense, so with that in mind what better way to start than by selecting a crystal intuitively.

TRAVEL H

GLOBAL SP

CAITLIN FLEMMING & JULIE GOEBEL
PHOTOGRAPHY BY PEGGY WONG

TRAVEL HOME

KATIE MOSS

Celebrations

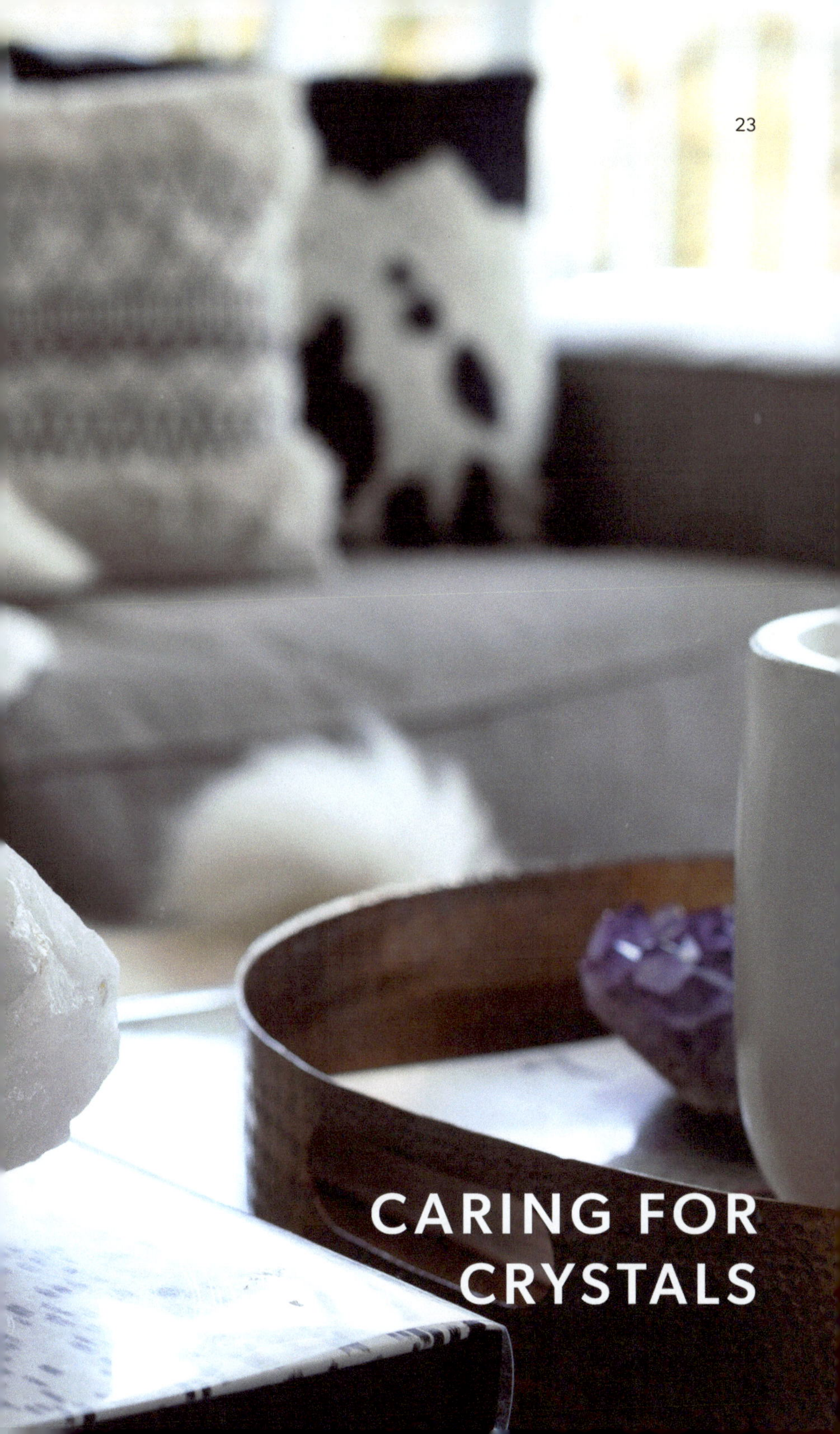

CARING FOR CRYSTALS

24

How to cleanse or charge a crystal.
It is said that crystals hold energy—be it good or bad—of the environment and people they encounter. When you bring your crystals home it is ideal to cleanse and reset their energy. As crystals tap into a universal energy source, they can assist you in areas such as meditation, manifestation and healing, but in theory they can tire just as we do after a busy week. Learning new ways to work with the crystals can also strengthen your relationship with them, alongside appreciating their ethereal beauty.

If you're interested in working with crystals to meditate, or programme with certain intentions, it's a good idea to cleanse them first and then to continue to charge them on a regular basis. There are some crystals that are considered superchargers (such as quartz, selenite and black obsidian) whereby they can charge other surrounding crystals. It's worth adding some of the dual-purpose crystals to your collection. Here are some ways for you to explore cleansing and charging your crystals.

Smudge.

Sageing your crystals is a great way to reset the energetic field. Burning sage is one of the oldest and purest methods of cleansing yourself and your home of any negative vibes. Just light it up and swirl the smoke around your crystal and your space. You can say intentions or incantations. The other benefit to smudging is it will make your home smell rich and earthy. I always find my space somehow feels a little lighter after this type of clearing. The same principal will apply when it comes to sageing your stones.

This cleansing process can also apply when using incense such as, palo santo, cedarwood and sandalwood.

Water.

You do have to be careful when using water on certain stones as too much exposure can damage the crystal itself. I do suggest a quick Google search prior to assist in the decision 'to wet or not to wet' your specimen. A rule of thumb is harder stones such as quartz fair better than the softer more delicate stone structures. Water itself is a wonderful clearing element and the idea is to quickly wash your stone to cleanse the crystal. The premise being that it will wash away any remanent energies the stone may have encountered along its path to you, and to leave the stone refreshed.

Earth.

Planting your crystal in the ground or soil is meant to recharge and cleanse it. The idea is to plant them for a day and allow the crystal to cleanse in a comfortable familiar environment. Do try to avoid treated soil where possible, and I strongly suggest some form of marker above ground, so you don't forget exactly where you buried your crystals.

Sun and Moon.
This is my favourite method to recharge and cleanse my stones.
Every full moon, I take a select few and place them outside so
the glow of the moon hits the crystals and cleanses and charges
them at the same time. I love collecting my stones the next
morning. They always feel cool to the touch and seem to have an
enhanced glisten after an evening under the moon and stars.

With sun cleansing, ensure your crystals get direct light for at least
four hours, but a small warning, crystals are reflective of light so don't
place them anywhere that may potentially start a fire. Also beware
that certain crystals can fade if they have too much sun exposure.

Sound.

Sound healing bowls such as Tibetan singing bowls are a powerful way to cleanse your stones. These bowls are also beautiful objects in their own right to add to your home decor and sound beautiful when chimed.

You can also play meditation music, or stream sound bowl compilations or recordings. The idea here is that the vibration of sound and frequency will restore the crystal to its clear and original state.

Salt.
Rock salt is a wonderful tool to cleanse
both yourself and your crystals. Think of
salt lamps, salt rooms and luxurious salt
baths, all of which are intended to purify
the body and your space. The same
idea applies to purifying crystals. Simply
bury your stones in a bed of sea salt or
Himalayan salt, let them cleanse for an
hour, then collect your renewed crystals.

SPIRITUAL
CONNECTION

PERFEC

STONE

ERFECT   *Karen McCartney / Sharyn Cairns / Glen Proebstel*

Meditation.

One of the most popular ways that people like to connect with crystals is to use them while meditating. Crystals have special powers. For example, amethyst can help with mental clarity, citrine can attract abundance, rose quartz can assist with love and clear quartz can be programmed to do all of the above. If you hold a stone while you are in a deep mental state, or place one on a part of your body that you are focusing on such as your temple, palm or chest, the energy of the crystal will do its work. You can also create a crystal grid or crystal circle and meditate within the space to amplify the crystal's power. Many meditation spaces have crystals by the door, near the window or on an altar. Just having them near you when you are tuning in or calming the mind can be beneficial to shift a room's energy—and yours!

Healing.

Crystals can be used for healing work in many ways, from chunks of rose quartz outside a day spa or massage parlour, to small clusters placed in the corners of healer's consult rooms. Each crystal has its own purpose and can also be grouped with other crystals to perform multiple functions. Crystals have the ability to be programmed with specific tasks or intentions that you may set for them. Crystals can assist in the curing of pains, aliments and illness. Whilst it is always recommended to seek medical guidance from your health care professional first, there is massive community of alternative healers who work with crystals and their healing powers. On a base level you could argue the placebo effect of having a stone with you as part of a healing path could be enough to lift your energy. Alternatively, if you believe crystals penetrate into your mind and soul and work on a frequency, you are sure to feel some benefit.

Here pictured is a chakra healing crystal star. Each of us have seven main chakra points within our bodies. These chakra points are the root chakra (red) situated at the base of your spine, the sacral chakra (orange) situated in your reproductive area, the solar plexus chakra (yellow) placed at your naval, the heart chakra (green) in your chest, the throat chakra (blue) in your throat, the third eye chakra (indigo) between your eyebrows and finally the crown chakra (lilac) at the top of your head. These points are considered divine energy points within each of us. They can be become blocked with emotional or psychical tension. A way to realign and clear your chakras is to work with crystals. Select crystals in the same associated colours to the chakra points and place the crystals on the desired chakra point and meditate or visualise clearing and healing of the chakra point.

Manifestation.
You can use crystals to help manifest goals and dreams, it's known as the Law of Attraction. A simple approach is to select a crystal associated with the desire you have, write a note to the universe, then place a crystal and a lit candle on top of the note and let the crystal work its magic. Crystals help get the message across to a universal energy, and let's face it … it just looks stunning twinkling in the candlelight.

There are many ways to do manifestation work: you can journal and set daily or weekly intentions. You can also meditate on your goals, or visualise your goals, along with affirmations or mantras. By choosing a few crystals to be part of these rituals, potentially you will supercharge your message.

Crystal Grids.

Crystal grids can be powerful tools, similar to manifesting work, it's all about your intentions. There are many ways to create crystal grids, you can use one stone type only, or mix stone types together for several purposes. The idea is that the crystal grid will amplify and magnify your intention and put it out to the universe. You can create star shapes, circles, layered rings, square or diamond shapes. If you're looking for guidance on grid types, Instagram or Pinterest are wonderful sources for crystal grid inspiration.

For example, you could create a grid to focus on specific chakra healing by using yellow stones if you are working on your solar plexus. You can create love grids with pink and green stones, for enlightenment grids try purple stones, or for confidence opt for blue stones. You can mix the colours and crystal types together for customised super grids. The options are limitless.

Altars.

I love incorporating crystals into altars in my home, much like grids the idea is to group stones that represent an intention or desire to you. Smokey quartz, black obsidian and black tourmaline work well if you are looking to cleanse your life of negative people or energy. If you are wanting general inspiration and direction, you can try grouping clear quartz stones together. Altars are fun to personalise to, you can include photos, feathers, or other found sentimental objects, experiment with items that are meaningful to your overall intention.

I am led by my visual senses as much as my emotional senses, so when I create a crystal altar, I will select crystals that complement each other visually. Let your eye fall over certain heights, shapes and textures, this will inspire and awaken a sense of calm or wonderment and pays a homage to the natural beauty of these creations.

Rituals.

It's hard to guide you on a specific ritual to follow, when it's such a personal form of expression and will depend on so many factors such as your belief system, life influences, cultural values, and your own personality. What I can offer, is that rituals can be as simple as returning home from a draining day and lighting a candle or playing some southing soul music. It could be as simple as holding a crystal which may help you decompress or allow your mind wonder to new solutions. A ritual is a personal practice. The beauty of working with crystals is there is no right or wrong way. Rituals are as precious and personal as your own sense of self, as your inner passions, as your spiritual or religious views. A ritual should be about your expression and experience of the wider world.

VOLUSPA

ROSE
COLORED
GLASSES

THE RELATABLE
CANDLE CO.

BUYING
THE
CAND

PHYSICAL
CONNECTION

Wear.
Wearing crystal jewellery is a way to start cultivating a crystal connection and collection. From rings, to necklaces, bracelets or earrings, there are endless options and many stunning creations that you can adorn your body with. Like the process of selecting a crystal piece, choose jewellery that catches your eye, colours that resonate and shapes that represent your personal aesthetic. You can mix many colours and crystals, they will not only beautify your presentation, they will silently do their work to protect and heal. It's a comforting thought, is it not?

Bathe.

Bathing is a wonderful way to energise, relax, recoup and recharge. A quiet night at home, candles flickering, bubbles foaming and crystals sparkling in the moody misty light. Having time in ritual such as a bath helps to destress and decompress and is important for our wellbeing. Bathing can promote mental clarity and aid your physical recovery. Choosing bath salts could be another book unto itself, it's a joy to try different blends, scents and combinations to submerse in, and so is choosing crystals to bring into your bathing routine. Surrounding yourself with pretty crystals alongside the act of soaking in salts is the perfect way to be in the present moment. Bathing is a remedy to release worry and calm the body.

INGREDIENTS

EPSOM SALT ·
FRENCH LAVENDER ·
HIBISCUS FLOWERS ·
RED ROSE PETALS ·
LAVENDER ESSENTIAL OIL ·

Warning: Some essential oils may cause irritation to allergic reactions in people with sensitive skin or if you wish to do a patch test before regular use

WWW.NINABAILEY.COM.AU

Sleep.

Sleep is as important as the food you nourish yourself with, the mindfulness you practice and how often you exercise and care for your body. Having a supportive crystal on your bedside, or a small stone under your pillow, can promote clearer dreams, deeper rest and cleansing for your mind and body—all whilst you sleep!

Protection.
Placing crystals in the main entry of your home is another way to feel supported. Crystals with their other worldly vibrations, can repel bad energy or vibes entering your home. I have a large amethyst cave at my front door, and it is not only a visual statement when people approach the house, it's also a great talking point and adds a welcoming magical feel to my entryway. You can select love or friendship stones, protective stones, abundance stones or even career focused stones. Any crystal that feels right to you is the one to place at your door, and it will also set the tone for your personal haven.

HOME CONNECTION

I'm a fan of giant oversized crystals clusters. They make an incredible statement and can instantly elevate your home and create a stunning focal point. With oversized pieces, I often style them simply on a side table of their own. You can also place them at the front door, or on the floor next to an occasional chair. These beauties will draw the eye and upscale elegance to any room. This piece is Himalayan quartz.

Gathering different coloured and
textured crystals on a brass tray
is a pretty way to display them,
and it's a great way to rotate your
favourite pieces or your working
crystals in a beautiful way. Pair
with candles for extra sparkle.

Selenite in a display box is
picture perfect. This is a nice
way to display any crystal
and evokes a whimsical
cabinet of curiosities feel.

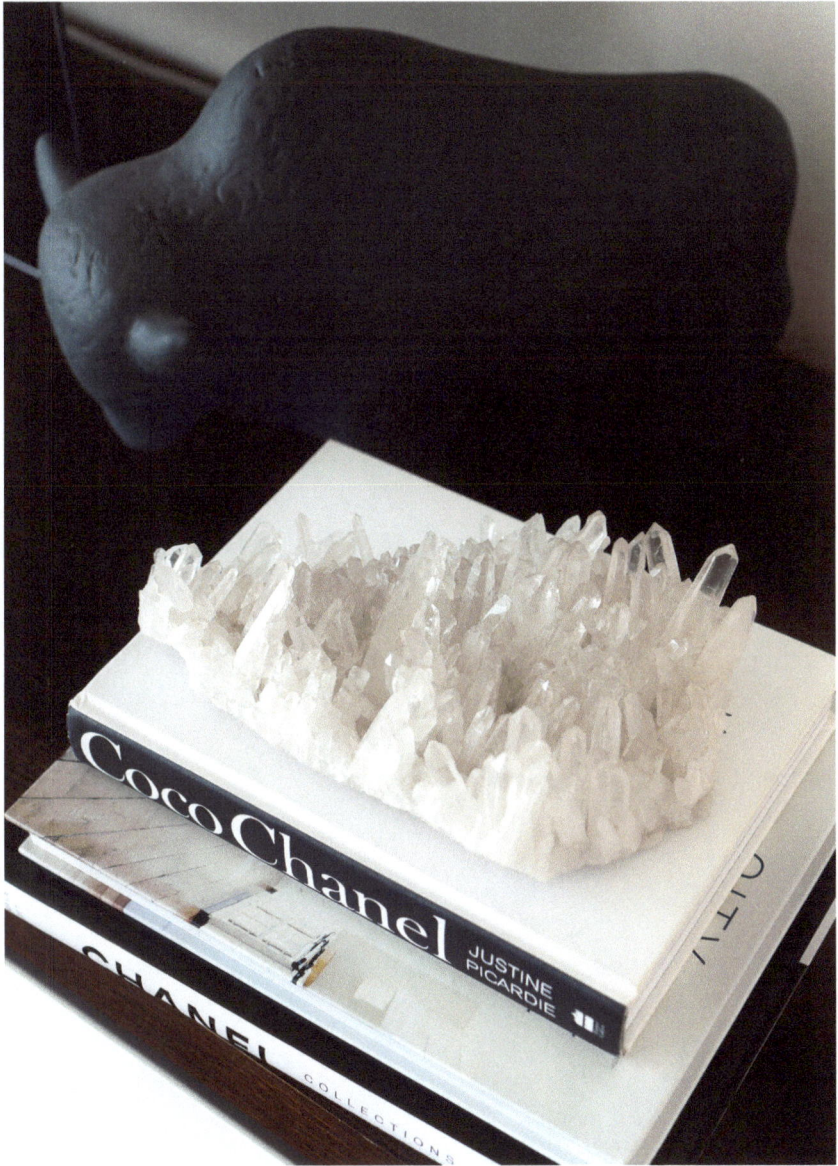

Style your larger clusters on a stack of books. I love collecting interior design, fashion and photography books. A large crystal piece will add a sculptural element to your book collection.

KATE M

Graphic textures and patterns work well with the opaque nature of many crystals, so don't be afraid to go bold with rugs, cushions and textiles. They won't compete, rather they will compliment.

The joy of selecting crystal pieces is that the shapes, points and formations are so varied from crystal to crystal. If you are going to grow a collection, look for shapes that you can play with in either shelves, tables or to group together. The more unique each piece is the more dramatic your display will be.

Position large clusters close to a natural light source and you will see the translucent quality of the crystal is amplified, it will cast different light tones at different times of the day. Crystals have gorgeous veining, inner formations, faceted faces and edges. With the changing daylight your crystal may look clear, cloudy or opaque.

Coffee table styling is a way to showcase a treasured crystal. Pair with metallic tones like brass, copper, gold and silver. Mixed metal tones pair beautifully with the textural quality of crystals.

Grouping a few large crystal clusters is another beautiful way to style a coffee or dining table. Alternate your crystals with candles and this will look incredible at night. When the lights dim, the twinkle and sparkle of the candlelight reflecting off the stones creates a magical setting.

Purchase crystals with beautiful graining and varied patterns. The intricate colours, lines and tones are so gorgeous, and they can stand alone as a beautiful decor item.

Consider grouping
coloured blooms
with matching tone
crystals to create a
stunning centrepiece.

Oversized candles and a pretty crystal cluster is a simple and winning recipe.

SANTAL 26 *intérieur*
1200g / 42.3 oz

scented candle / bougie parfumée

Hand poured in USA - **LE LABO** - 233 Elizabeth Street, NYC 10012

Bookshelf styling will instantly be elevated by the inclusion of earthly elements such as coral, driftwood, shells and crystals.

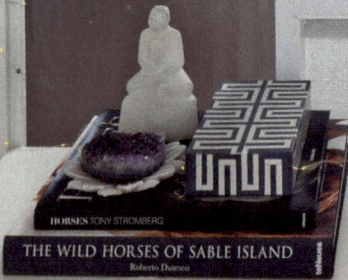

Create little scenes or moments on your shelves. These mini displays tell a story about the treasures and items you collect. Alternate these items with a selection of sentimental pictures or prints, decorative vessels and books for a visually interesting, layered overall presentation.

Simple monochromatic styling elements such as books in neutral tones will not detract from your crystals, rather they will enhance your collection and create a platform from which to display them.

My Dog's Territory book, Series 8   Sydney Dogs   Photography by Pierre Mardaga

The trick with any bookshelf styling
is to leave white or blank spaces,
allow your objects and crystals room
to become the central focus with a
visual space surrounding them.

Agate bookends are a pretty way to incorporate crystals into your space. They are available in many colours and sizes and will highlight all your favourite reads.

Grouping a few smaller crystal items
with varying vessels and vases is a more
dramatic way to showcase them.

HOME

A HAVEKES PHOTOGRAPHY BY ANDREW LEHMANN

MOSS

Coral clusters and crystal clusters were made for each other. Adding crystal caves will also add dimension to your shelf decor.

Hollywood Unseen
With a foreword by Joan Collins

HARLEY-DAVIDSON
THE LEGENDARY MODELS
PASCAL SZYMEZAK

Twinkle lights weaved through
coral and crystals looks
magical as the lights dim.

The neutral tones of the grouped crystal cave, clusters and coral chunks create texture, depth and dimension, even though the overall tones are very soft.

Mixing crystal points, slices and clusters on any surface will create a visual feast. The different shapes and heights work in harmony to create visual interest.

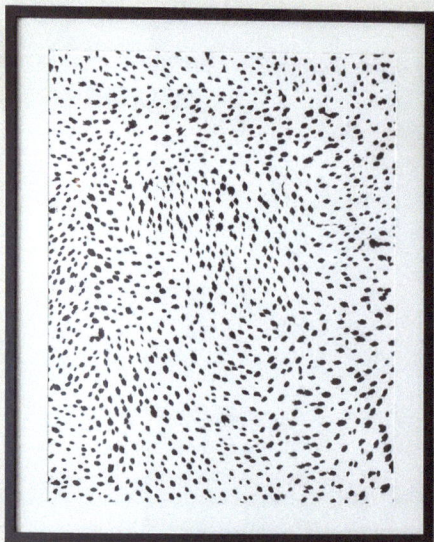

Crystals will work on any furniture surface and can all be harnessed to display different crystal elements. You can place crystals anywhere there is a visual gap as most crystals are translucent or opaque, they do not look overpowering.

With bookshelf styling, I suggest crystals alternating on every shelf, but somehow, they don't really ever compete. They seem to work well as a whole collection, creating a feeling of visual unison overall.

A crystal trinket box paired with a vintage glass paperweight
and a milky quartz piece create a nice moment.

A bowl of selenite balls reflects light and creates an ever changing fluid artwork.

Clear quartz is a super crystal and can be programmed for many functions. Oversize clusters are my favourite to collect and display, their glimmering clear beauty has no comparison. They remind me of snow or ice, which creates a sense of childhood nostalgia and whimsy to any space.

Mini trinket dishes or small bowls are the perfect place for keeping your small crystal collections.

Display your crystal treasure on wooden boards to elevate and create interesting visual layers.

Stone busts and statues add a beautiful classic and elegant feel to your home. When you combine with glittering crystals, it delights the senses and can make your space feel like a fairytale setting.

Sculptural florals such as orchids complement crystal clusters beautifully.

Celestite will be sure to make any surface shine. Crystals and plants are lovely when grouped close together.

Display crystals in your kitchen. Group with pretty glass canisters or stoneware for an eye-catching moment.

Thames & Hudson

COZY
white
COTTAGE

100 WAYS TO LOVE
THE FEELING OF BEING HOME

LIZ MARIE
GALVAN

the VINTAGE TEA PARTY book

Crystal coasters and bottle openers will jazz up your bar car or drinks area.

This pyrite piece on a stand glistens next to marble trinket boxes.

Using crystal slabs or trays for grazing boards is a beautiful way to impress your guests.

House a favourite candle or potted plant with crystals.

Crystals, books and textured or metallic trays work together every time.

Don't be afraid to play with scale, colour and texture. There are no rules! The key is to display crystal pieces you love.

128

Calcite cave halves can be split when decorating, one on a bookshelf, one on a side table, two pretty moments for the price of one.

Calcite, coral and quartz when grouped in three tell a
beautiful story and add a point of interest to a hall table.

Crystal serving ware will make
any dinner party sparkle.

Consider using crystal place card holders to create a beautiful table scape. It will assist in creating a magical evening for your guests too.

GRUAU PORTRAITS OF M

ELEMENTAL LIV

Raw crystal chunks look just as pretty as
polished clusters, their earthy rough texture
makes them perfect pieces to display.

Crystal caves, floral arrangements
and coral are wonderful items to
use when dressing a side table.

Cloudy crystals are beautiful.
When placed near a light
source they emit a soft surreal
glow. Little crystal caves
create little visual delights.

Textural over scale candle sticks look stunning right next to crystal pieces or crystal clusters.

Rich jewel toned crystals will add a sense of warm to your rooms
or centrepieces. Here we have citrine and calcite.

Selenite candle votives and a citrine piece sit well on a vintage bench which
I have repurposed here instead of choosing a standard console table.

Crystals have a calming effect on our beloved pets, consider setting a small stone under a dog or cat bed, hang a crystal pendant near a bird cage, or tie a tiny crystal to their name tag.

Crystal shapes make wonderful, pretty styling
objects. For an extra visual punch try layering on
trays or platters to create a dramatic backdrop,
this works to frame your crystal piece.

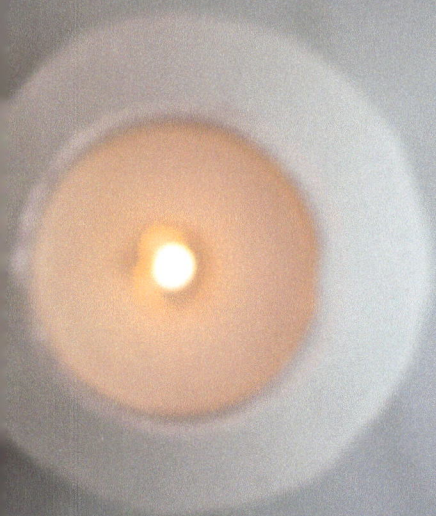

Salt lamps, candles and mini
altars work well together.

SAND + FOG

CRISP
WHITE

MADE WITH
ESSENTIAL OILS

at 100

Place a crystal cluster alongside sentimental
objects and candles, and you have an
instant altar and decorative vignette.

Rose quartz is a beloved stone, raw chunks are beautifully organic and wonderful tools to include in your styling.

Mini caves and found objects make a beautiful pairing.

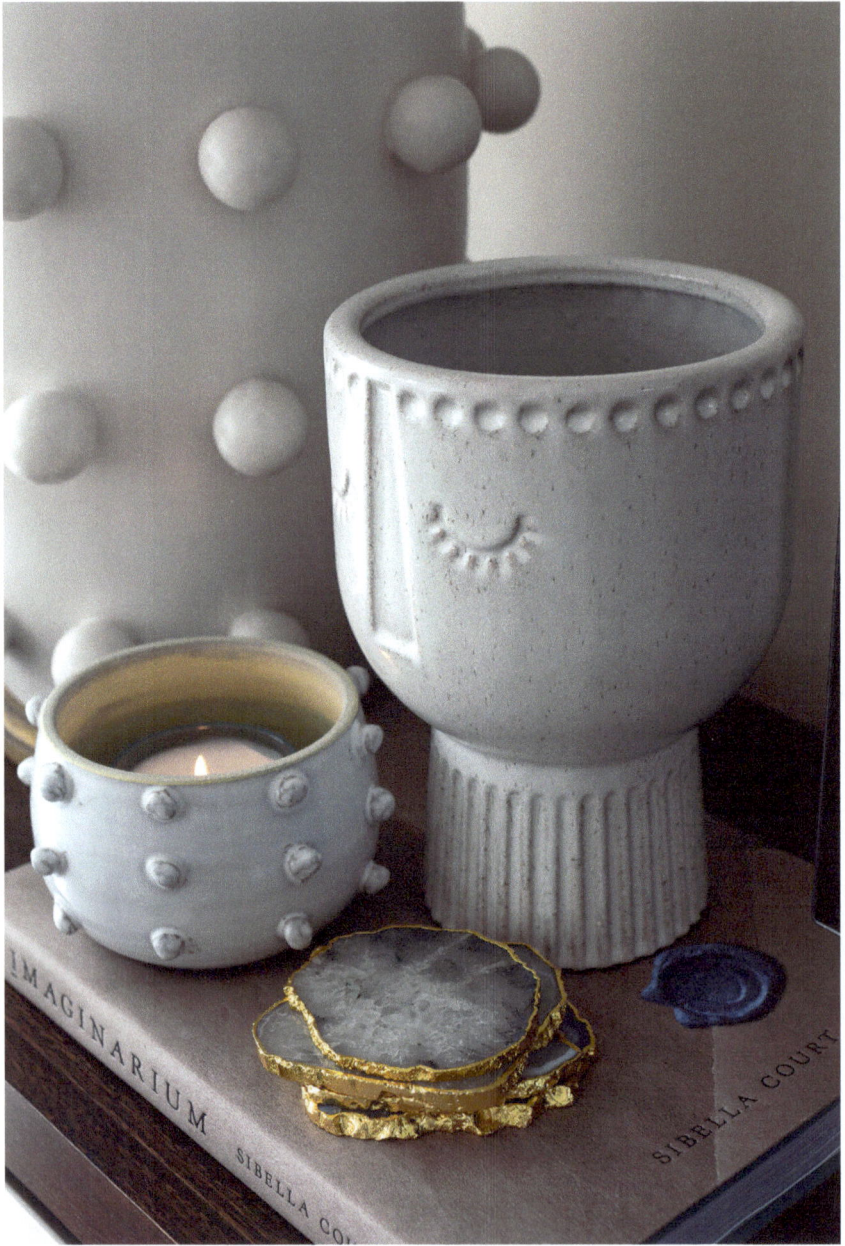

Agate coasters make pretty decor on their own.

walton

Lonnie Wurtz Jensen

Muscovite mica is a stunning rock. It has a natural metallic
shine and catches the light beautifully, as do many crystals.

TASCHEN

Hematoid quartz has a lovely peachy warm tone and sits well with a mercury glass vase, and a neutral candle. They are all visually united by the base tray.

Pampas grass and quartz votives evoke a relaxed day spa like feel.

Amethyst flower is a beautiful
crystal to display on a stand,
so you can appreciate the
intricate formations.

Standing crystals
make wonderful
decorative accents.

Play with different objects, shapes and materials
and sizes to enrich your crystal vignettes.

Crystal spheres look pretty
when grouped in a series.

Coloured agate bookends
on top of books is a
nice decorative twist.

There is something about brass and crystals together! Add some marble and you can't go wrong.

Pyrite chunks are beautiful
when grouped together.

Malachite animals will bring the cute factor to your space.

Lots of tiny crystal fragments together tell an exciting visual story.

Crystals and tarot nights are good for the soul. Having a few smaller crystal items at hand can assist in creating a magical evening.

Little details create little magical moments in your home. Small crystal surprises within shelves or bowls is a nice way to place your items.

Treasures that have been collected, gathered or foraged placed alongside crystals will create a beautiful eclectic display.

Books and crystals work together, turn the spines around, this allows the crystal to shine front and centre.

When crystals are featured
in your home and when the
light hits just the right place,
you will be transported
to a mythical place.

I hope this little book has provided some new ideas on how to play with your special stones. Collecting crystals, and finding new ways to work with them, incorporate them and showcase them has been wonderful therapy for me, and hopefully an enjoyable visual journey for you. I hope you now feel motivated and inspired to start your own *crystal connection.*

JXX

CRYSTAL RESOURCES

RECOMMENDED READING

The Crystal Bible: A Definitive Guide to Crystals by Judy Hall

The Power of Crystal Healing: Change Your Energy And Live A High-Vibe Life by Emma Lucy Knowles

Crystals: The modern guide to crystal healing by Yulia Van Doren

Crystals: Everything You Need to Know to Heal. Cleanse. Love. Energize by Cassandra Eason

The Crystal Directory: 100 Crystals for Positive Manifestation by Sarah Bartlett

ORACLE AND TAROT DECKS

The crystal oracle by Toni Carmine Salerno

Uusi - Pagan Otherworlds Tarot

CRYSTAL SHOPPING GUIDE

naturesenergy.com.au

mineralism.com.au

sourceressthestore.com.au

stonedcrystals.com

crystalcastle.com.au

therockcrystalshop.com.au

thesocietyinc.com.au

hetties.co.nz

rozellecrystals.business.site

unearthedcrystals.com.au

Instagram: crystals_of_australia

THE CRYSTAL VAULT GLOSSARY

Agate: a grounding stone to promote maturity and stability

Amethyst: mental clarity and spiritual connection, an easy to source stone

Beryl: a calming stone that will assist in motivation

Calcite: cleanser of energy and psychical healing

Carnelian: attracts success and abundance

Celestine: prayer and mindfulness, focus, mediation

Citrine: abundance, wealth success and positive vibes

Clear quartz: the master stone, can be programmed for any function

Labradorite: a protective stone, restores energy,
assists balance, reveals true emotions

Malachite: protection from electronic rays, protection when travelling

Moldavite: a rare and powerful stone, healing for the heart and mind

Moonstone: to strengthen psychic abilities, inner wisdom and dream work

Pyrite: psychic connection and channelling, mental stability

Rose quartz: a crystal that promotes love and self-love in all forms

Rutilated quartz: heal all your chakras, a divine stone to meditate with

Selenite: to assist in cleansing other crystals

Smokey quartz: a protective stone, absorbs bad intentions, restore your confidence

Sodalite: a stone for self-expression, enhancing intuition, to assist spiritual growth

Tigers eye: sharpen the senses and attract good fortune and luck

Turquoise: a purification stone, heals the whole body, wards anxiety and panic

AUTHOR'S NOTE

I fell in love with crystals when I was a child, and began collecting them in my late twenties, after a trip to New Zealand. It was there I discovered the magic of a crammed and crowded, bursting crystal shop. With so many wonders to explore, and beautiful pieces available, I came home with a suitcase full of crystal objects and have since built my collection piece by piece. Every year I add a few more clusters and now my home is positively vibrating with crystals (there is barely a surface that's doesn't showcase at least one!).

I have a deep love and connection to the idea of 'home'. I truly believe the space you reside in has an immediate impact on your feelings, sense of self, and energy. Creating beautiful spaces is not only my career, but my obsession and I have a passion for incorporating crystals within my own sacred space. The hunt for beautiful crystals is an ongoing love affair, addiction and favoured pastime.

From a personal perspective, whilst I do certainly have a blessed life, like all of us, I have faced my own hardships and traumas. I lost both my parents before the age of 30, I have chronic back pain from a spinal injury, I was diagnosed with Crohn's disease (the same illness my mother struggled with), and I endured a marriage breakdown. I was diagnosed with PTSD from a traumatic health incident brought on by all these episodes which exhausted me and shattered me physically and mentally. Suffice to say, I hit my lowest point, feeling overwhelmed with depression and anxiety and feeling lost and directionless.

It's important to note that I certainly do not think my journey has been any harder than anyone else's, I share my own personal story only to shed light on the belief that we should all practice empathy and kindness (as you never really know what anyone else is going through!). Understanding that we as humans all endure tough times throughout our lives, be it grief, heartache, illness, work or social pressures, or all of the above.

On a positive note, I do believe that we are ultimately in control of our own lives and have the ability to overcome obstacles and hardships. Like a phoenix that must rise from the ashes to be reborn, there is always something to learn from the dark periods, and we are as resilient as we are vulnerable. I held onto the belief that things would get better, looked for miracles, magic and beauty, and always kept going, one step in front of the other. I started my interior design and property styling business 'Vault Interiors' at age 27, which has grown into a bustling business where we style up to 700 homes a year. I have three beautiful rescue Pomeranians, and wonderful support from family, friends and my staff. Through all these times, I have come to depend on the healing quality of my home without question. It is a sacred space to retreat, to recharge, and that is a true reflection of my life and my story.

The more crystals that I have acquired, the more my space feels energised and as a result I feel energised, motivated and excited for the future. I believe in the healing properties, in conjunction with modern medicine, which has also assisted me—it is a perfect balance. With crystals surrounding me and a positive mindset I feel confident to carry on through the ebbs and flows that is life.

I owe a lot to crystals, they inspire and comfort me, and they beautify my space. So, I do hope this book gives you a glimpse into my own personal *crystal connection* and inspires you to explore your own connection.

FOR MORE DAILY INSPIRATION
 FOLLOW MY JOURNEY ON:
Instagram (the book) @crystalconnectionbook
Instagram (personal) @justbeen16
Instagram (business) @vaultinteriors
www.vaultinteriors.com.au